TOP SPEEDS

HORSE — 75 KM (46 MILES) PER HOUR

ELECTRIC SKATEBOARD — 37 KM (23 MILES) PER HOUR

DOG — 70 KM (43.5 MILES) PER HOUR

BULLET TRAIN — 350 KM (220 MILES) PER HOUR

NOW THAT'S FAST!: BULLET TRAINS

RABBIT — 72 KM (45 MILES) PER HOUR

HUMAN — 45 KM (28 MILES) PER HOUR

BIKE — 132 KM (82 MILES) PER HOUR

NOW THAT'S FAST!

BULLET TRAINS

KATE RIGGS

W
FRANKLIN WATTS
LONDON • SYDNEY

First published in the UK in 2011 by
Franklin Watts
338 Euston Road
London NW1 3BH

Franklin Watts Australia
Level 17/207 Kent Street
Sydney NSW 2000

First published by Creative Education,
an imprint of the Creative Company.

ISBN 978 1 4451 0585 7
Dewey number: 625.2

A CIP catalogue record for this book
is available from the British Library.

Printed in China

Franklin Watts is a division of
Hachette Children's Books,
an Hachette UK company.
www.hachette.co.uk

Book and cover design by Blue Design
(www.bluedes.com)
Art direction by Rita Marshall

Photographs by Corbis (Patrick Bennett, Bettmann),
Dreamstime (Gvision, Sportslibrary), Getty
Images (PATRICK HERTZOG/AFP, Simeone Huber,
FRANCISCO LEONG/AFP, JEFF PACHOUD/AFP,
Piotr Powietrzynski, Quinn Rooney, Martin Rose/
Bongarts, Topical Press Agency), iStockphoto
(Arthur Achtelik)
Every atttempt has been made to clear copyright.
Should there be any inadvertent omission, please
contact the publisher for rectification.

A bullet train is a high-speed **passenger** train. Bullet trains are the fastest trains in the world. Most bullet trains travel at average speeds of around 250–300 kilometres per hour (kph).

Some of the most famous bullet trains are in Japan. Here a bullet train speeds past Mount Fuji.

Bullet trains are used to carry people from place to place. Some bullet trains carry **freight**, too. Most bullet trains run on electricity. This means that they are better for the **environment** than other trains, which use a fuel called **diesel**. Using diesel creates **pollution** and contributes to **global warming**.

All bullet trains have parts called **locomotives**. These are engines that pull or push the train along. They are on each end of the train. Between the two locomotives are the train cars where passengers sit. The longest trains have 16 to 18 cars.

People board, or get on, a bullet train when it stops at a station.

A driver controls and steers the bullet train. Bullet trains run on special tracks. The tracks are used only by bullet trains so that they do not get held up behind slower trains. The tracks are straight and smooth.

The driver sits in a small space in the front of the locomotive.

The first bullet train ran in Japan in 1964. It travelled between the cities of Tokyo and Osaka. The train was called the Shinkansen. Today, the modern Shinkansen carries over 150 million passengers a year at speeds of around 270 kph.

The Shinkansen was nicknamed a 'bullet train' because it travelled very fast.

French bullet trains run from Paris to cities all over Europe.

Today, there are bullet trains in China and across Europe. In France, bullet trains are known as TGV (*train à grande vitesse*, or very fast trains).

A TGV train called the Eurostar connects cities in England, Belgium and France. There is a sea called the English Channel between France and England. The Eurostar travels under the Channel in a tunnel. The tunnel is over 50 kilometres long.

Eurostar trains at St Pancras Station in London.

When a bullet train zooms

along the smooth tracks at top

speed, it can be hard to see.

It goes so fast that it is a blur!

It does not stop until

it reaches a station.

Bullet trains are built to be strong.
They can travel in almost any weather.

The driver makes sure that the bullet train reaches its destination safely and on time. Passengers cannot wait to travel on a super-fast bullet train again!

Fast Facts

In California in the USA, there are plans to build a bullet train to connect the cities of San Francisco and Los Angeles.

Some Spanish bullet AVE *(Alto Velocidad Española)* trains are nicknamed 'Ducks' because the front of the train looks like a duck's beak.

A bullet train in China goes at 300 kph every day. It is the fastest train in daily use.

A bullet train in France set a speed record in 2007. It reached a top speed of 574 kph!

Glossary

diesel – a fuel made from oil

environment – surroundings

freight – things that are carried on a train or other vehicle, such as post from a post office

global warming – a gradual increase in the Earth's temperature.

locomotives – the engines of the train. They push or pull the train along

passenger – someone who travels on a train or other vehicle

pollution – making the air, water or soil dirty

record –when something gives the best (or worst) performance, such as the fastest train

Read More about It

Fast! Bullet Trains by Ian Graham (QED Publishing, 2010)

Website

Kids Web Japan: Bullet Train
http://web-japan.org/kidsweb/hitech/shinkansen/index.html
This site explores the Japanese Shinkansen bullet trains.

Index